Pebble® Plus

Patterns in Nature

Phases of the Moon

by Gillia M. Olson

Consulting Editor: Gail Saunders-Smith, PhD

Consultant: Dr. Ronald Browne, Associate Professor of Elementary Education
Minnesota State University, Mankato, Minnesota

Capstone press®

Mankato, Minnesota

Pebble Plus is published by Capstone Press,
1710 Roe Crest Drive, North Mankato, Minnesota 56003.
www.capstonepub.com

Library of Congress Cataloging-in-Publication Data
Olson, Gillia M.
  The phases of the moon / by Gillia Olson.
  p. cm. —(Pebble plus. Patterns in nature)
  Includes bibliographical references and index.
  ISBN-13: 978-0-7368-6340-7 (hardcover)
  ISBN-10: 0-7368-6340-0 (hardcover)
  ISBN-13: 978-0-7368-9617-7 (softcover pbk.)
  ISBN-10: 0-7368-9617-1 (softcover pbk.)
  1. Moon—Phases—Juvenile literature. 2. Pattern perception—Juvenile literature. I. Title. II. Series.
QB588.O47 2007
523.3′2—dc22   2006001454

Summary: Simple text and photographs introduce moon phases, including why they occur and what they
    are called.

Editorial Credits
Heather Adamson, editor; Kia Adams, designer; Renée Doyle, illustrator; Jo Miller, photo researcher;
    Scott Thoms, photo editor

Photo Credits
Corbis/Richard Cummins, 10–11; Mike Zens, 12–13; zefa/Frans Lemmens, cover (full moon with city)
Index Stock Imagery/Ken Wardius, 14–15
Nature Places Library/Artur Tabor, 16–17, 18–19
Peter Arnold/Werner H. Muller, 5
Photodisc, cover (moon)
Photo Researchers Inc./Gerard Lodriguss, 8–9
Shutterstock/Vladimir Ivanov, backcover; Taipan Kid, 21 (all); Wayne James, 1
Unicorn Stock photos/Ed Harp, cover (moon with trees)

Note to Parents and Teachers

The Patterns in Nature set supports national science standards related to earth and
life science. This book describes and illustrates moon phases. The images support
early readers in understanding the text. The repetition of words and phrases helps early
readers learn new words. This book also introduces early readers to subject-specific
vocabulary words, which are defined in the Glossary section. Early readers may need
assistance to read some words and to use the Table of Contents, Glossary, Read More,
Internet Sites, and Index sections of the book.

Printed in the United States of America in North Mankato, Minnesota.
0602015
008999R

Table of Contents

The Moon's Shape

The moon seems

to change shape.

It doesn't.

The change is how much

of the moon you can see.

The sun lights up one side
of the moon.
The moon circles the Earth.
Your view of the moon changes.
From Earth, you see different
moon phases.

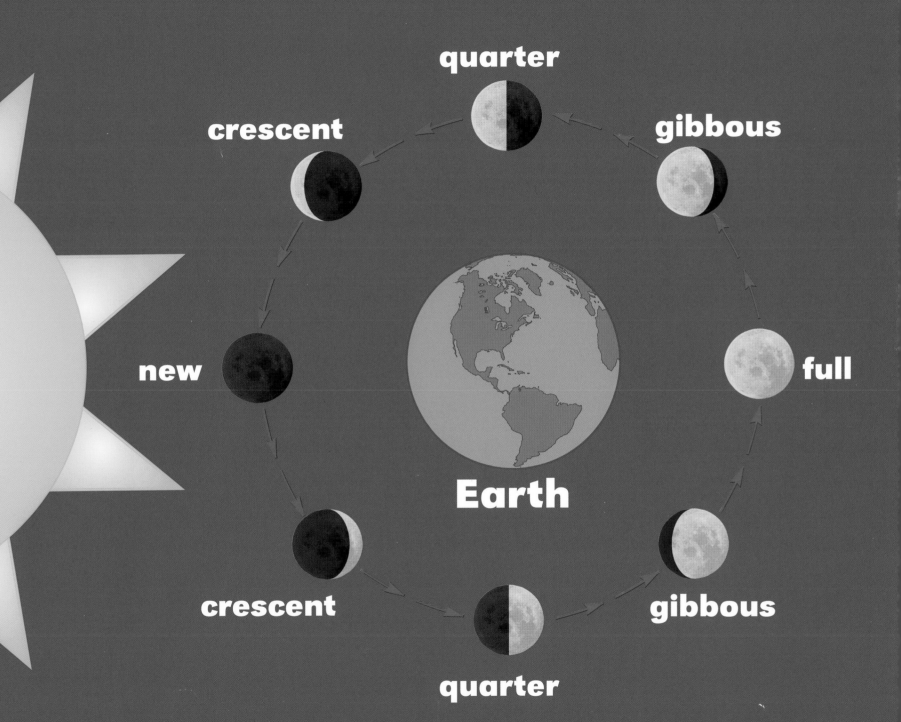

quarter

crescent

gibbous

new

Earth

full

crescent

quarter

gibbous

Moon Phases

The moon phases start
with the new moon.
The new moon looks all dark.
A few days later a small
sliver of moon appears.

The next phase
looks like a banana.
It's called a crescent moon.

Then the moon looks
like half of a circle.
This phase is a quarter moon.

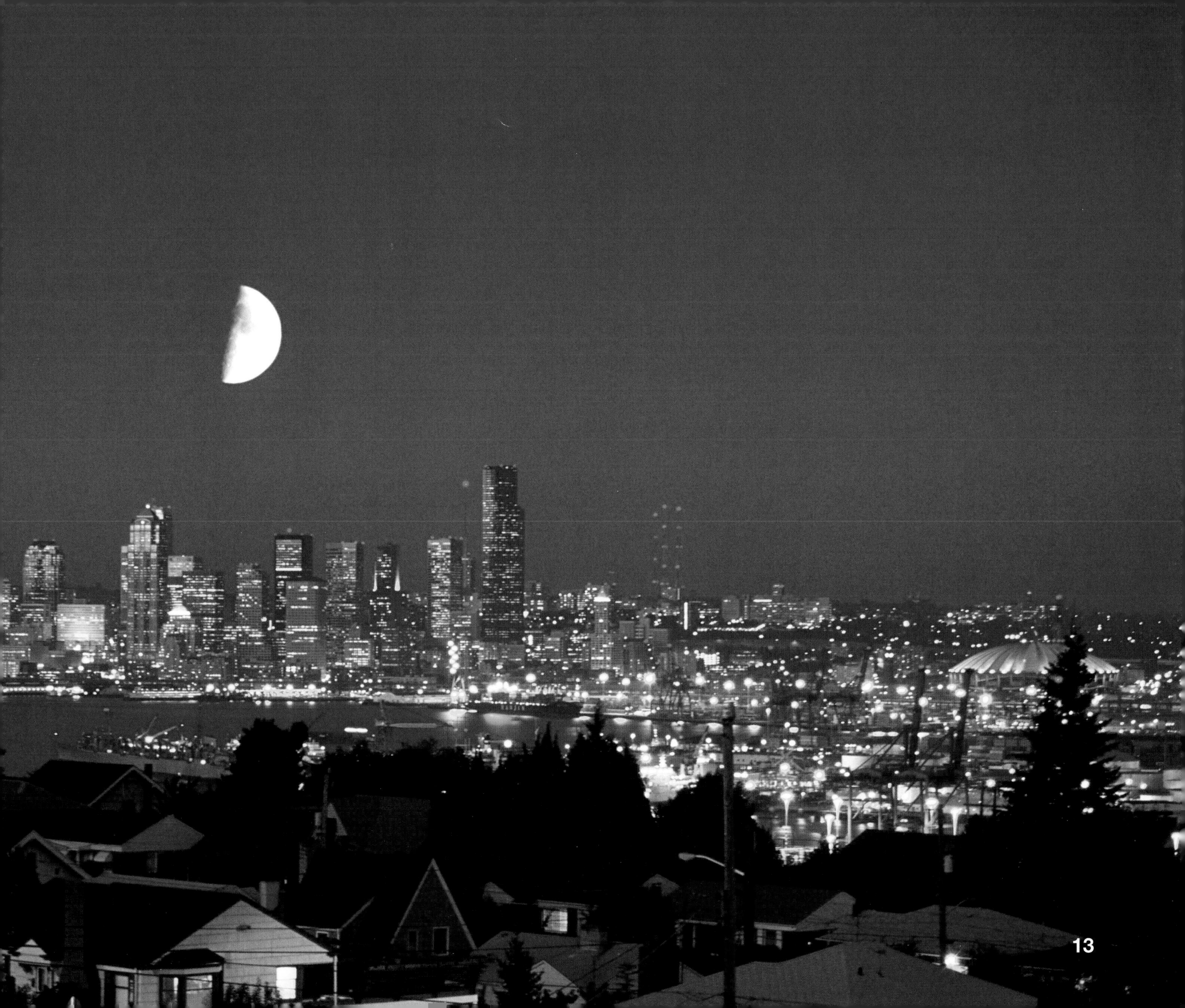

The next phase is
a gibbous moon.
It looks like a circle
with a crescent cut out.

15

Next, you see all
of the sunlit side.
It is a full moon.

It's a Pattern

After a full moon,
you see less and less
of the sunlit side.
Then, there is
a new moon again.

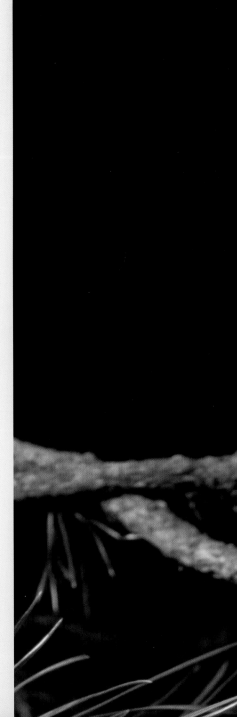

One after another,
all the moon phases
repeat each month.
The phases are one
of nature's patterns.

Glossary

Earth—the planet where we live; the moon is about 239,000 miles (385,000 kilometers) from Earth.

nature—everything in the world that isn't made by people

pattern—something that happens again and again in the same order

phase—a stage; the moon's phases are the shapes that it appears to take over a month.

sun—a star that gives the moon and earth light and warmth; a star is a large ball of burning gases in space.

sunlit—lit up by the sun

view—what you can see from a certain place; views change when you move and when objects, like the moon, move.

Read More

Bresden, Carmen. *The Moon.* Rookie Read-about Science. New York: Children's Press, 2003.

Rustad, Martha E. H. *The Moon.* Out in Space. Mankato, Minn.: Capstone Press, 2002.

Internet Sites

FactHound offers a safe, fun way to find Internet sites related to this book. All of the sites on FactHound have been researched by our staff.

Here's how:

1. Visit *www.facthound.com*

2. Choose your grade level.

3. Type in this book ID **0736863400** for age-appropriate sites. You may also browse subjects by clicking on letters, or by clicking on pictures and words.

4. Click on the **Fetch It** button.

FactHound will fetch the best sites for you!

Index

Word Count: 164
Grade: 1
Early-Intervention Level: 15